CONNECTOMICS

CONNECTOMICS

POEMS OF THE BRAIN

Alison Calder

First published 2017 by IRON Press
5 Marden Terrace
Cullercoats
North Shields
NE30 4PD
tel/fax +44(0)191 2531901
ironpress@blueyonder.co.uk
www.ironpress.co.uk

ISBN 978-0-9931245-9-4
Printed by Ingram Lightning Source
Typeset in Georgia 11 pt

Poems © Alison Calder 2017

IRON Press Books are distributed by NBN International
and represented by Inpress Ltd, 12 Mosley Street
Newcastle upon Tyne, NE1 1DE
Tel: 44(0) 191 2308104
www.inpressbooks.co.uk

CONTENTS

Foreword by Raymond Tallis	7
Connectomics	11
Clarity	12
C. elegans	14
Silent synapse	16
Infinity	18
Science	20
Functional Specialization	22
A Love Poem: Hebb's Postulate	23
Glia	24
Semantic Selectivity	26
Natural Narrative	28
Engram	30
Synaptic Cleft	31
Trials	32
Wellbutrin™	34
Flattened Cortex	36
Pycortex	38
Neuroinformatics	39
Optogenetics	40
Chimera	42
Chimera 2	44
"The Greater Mystery"	46
Chlamydomonas reinhardtii	48

Alison Calder

ALISON CALDER's first poetry collection, *Wolf Tree*, won two Manitoba Book Awards and was shortlisted for two Canadian national awards. Her second book, *In the Tiger Park*, was a finalist for the Lansdowne Prize. She collaborated with Jeanette Lynes on the chapbook *Ghost Works: Improvisations in Letters and Poems*. Some poems in the present collection first appeared in a limited edition, illustrated chapbook (with design by Lisa Johnson).

Alison was born in London and grew up in Saskatoon, Saskatchewan, Canada. She lives in Winnipeg, where she is a Professor in the Department of English, Film, and Theatre at the University of Manitoba.

Foreword

THERE IS A FASCINATING THOUGHT EXPERIMENT BELOVED OF PHILOSOPHERS. Imagine a device – called an 'autocerebroscope' – which enabled you to see the activity in your brain displayed on a screen. You could look at the nerve impulses corresponding to your looking at, and seeing, your nerve impulses. Leaving aside the ambiguities in the thought experiment, would you be looking at your looking? More precisely, would you be seeing your seeing? The answer is of course no. What you would be seeing on the screen would be trains of spikes and that would be nothing like what it is to see a train of spikes.

The autocerebroscope experiment highlights a gap that can never be closed between subjective experience and that which is observed objectively. This is reflected in the division between the scientific approach to the world which is objective and quantitative and general and the approach of the artist which respects our subjectivity, tries to capture the quality and singularity of experiences, and usually gives numbers and measurements a miss.

All of which is a roundabout way of saying why the wonderfully articulated, poised, often epigrammatic poems in Alison Calder's *Connectomics* – picking up glints from the cutting edge of neuroscience – are so beguiling. She asks us to look at our brains (and implicitly ourselves and our lives, our forgotten and remembered pasts) through the lens of bioscience refracted in turn through the mind of the poet. They are playful, witty, wry and often poignant.

Calder's erudition does not present an obstacle to the reader because she has the courtesy to explain things that may be unfamiliar in footnotes that are miracles of concision. Indeed, they make *Connectomics* into a dialogue between languages:

between the language of neuroscience, and that of imagination, nourished by memory, that strays far beyond the intracranial terrain of neuroscience.

Poetry, as Mallarmé famously said, is not made of ideas but of words and Calder is clearly in love with the language of bioscience. 'Synapse', 'glia', 'engram', 'optogenetics', are woven into her response to a discipline that is exceeded in mystery only by the brain it studies. In a perfect little poem, the neologisms in 'Chimera' are themselves chimeric constructions, doing what she is saying.

Occasionally she sounds a note of healthy scepticism. When she says

> *We grew our knowledge right up to the end.*
> *When we got to the limit, we stopped.*

we know not to take this at face value. She is smiling at the claims of some scientists that they will one day know all there is to know about us because they will have a full account of how the brain is wired up.

Connectomics is an autocerebroscope that will expand your mind. It does exactly what its title says: it makes connections – between languages, between cultures, and between ourselves and the brains that make it possible for us to be, know, and to make connections. And making connections is what above all poetry is, or should be, about.

Raymond Tallis
Liverpool 2017

CONNECTOMICS

Connectomics[1]

The idea is
to render the brain
transparent enough to read through,
like trickles of water washing away thought.

Deletions, insertions, translocations, inversions,
proofreaders' symbols carve a straight line
to the minotaur.

In the light of the laboratory,
thought's skein unravels,
bumpy road smoothing.

Lucent, pellucid, the brain wavers
like the glass in a display case,
minimum interference between eye and page.

Like reading through a jellyfish.
The text, however, remains opaque.

---

[1] Roughly speaking, the goal of connectomics is to improve ways to map the neural connections in the brain.

CLARITY[2]

Firefly mouse flickers, forgets
lessons, forgets
want. Inside his skull
the past incinerates, embers
blizzarding into ash.
The screened brain's a maze,
sizzling, fragments
of a film that's not replayed.
What and *how* and *why* flash briefly,
die. Mouse mind flares.
It turns to glass.

---

[2] CLARITY is the name of the process by which the brain is made transparent. Splicing firefly genes into mice makes neural mapping easier because parts of the brain will fluoresce. These mice are particularly used for Alzheimer's research.

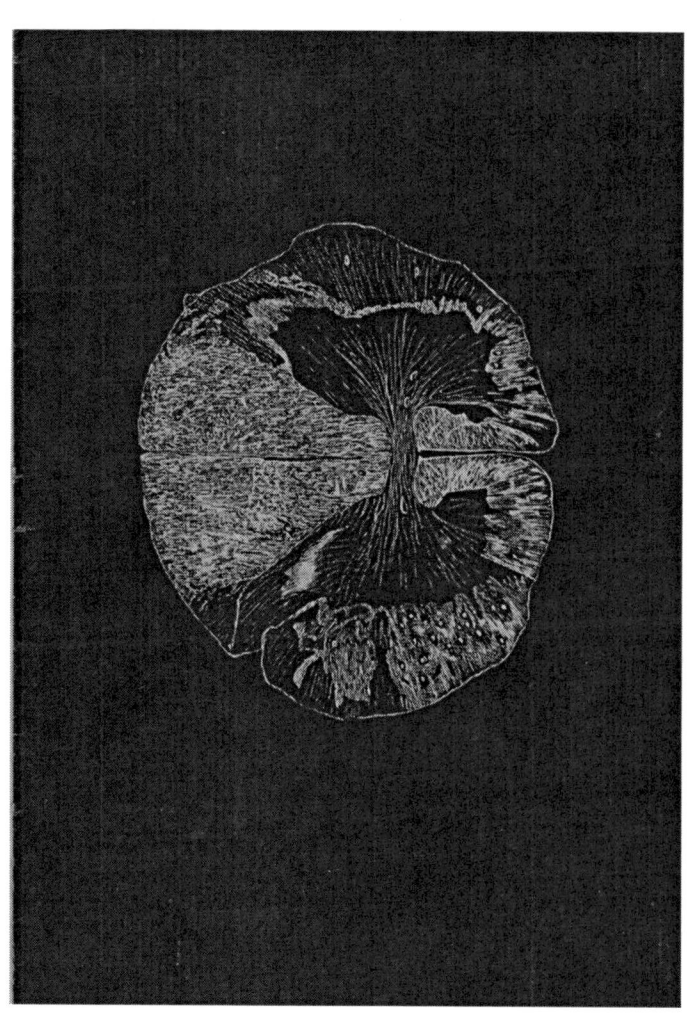

C. ELEGANS[3]

You call us simple.
On TV, innocents scream at cartoon germs,
brandish cleansers, scrub us away.
Grade six science classes learn what's living
in their lashes, are traumatized for life.
Still, I have what you need.
Complicated, tractable, I am the ideal
compromise between *like* and *not*.
I'm useful because I die quickly:
your funding agencies approve.
Plumbing for secrets in my glassy body,
you peer through my window
seeking 40 percent of your soul.
How age? How sleep? How want?
—the fundamental mysteries of biology
hidden in plain sight.

The manual says, "keep your samples separate from your
culture."
But let me reverse your gaze, turn
the microscope upon the viewer.
My elegant curves, the symmetries
of my crystalline motility, are mesmerizing.
Rotund, rotating, I root into regions
you've not been to. My eyeless face recognizes light.
Hermaphrodite, I love myself.
Non-hazardous, non-infectious, non-pathogenic, non-parasitic,
of no economic importance, I'm nothing
that you are.

---

[3] *Caenorhabditis elegans*, a small, soil-dwelling nematode, was the first animal to have its genome completely sequenced. 40 percent of its genome is identical to that of humans. All 959 somatic cells of its transparent body are visible in a microscope.

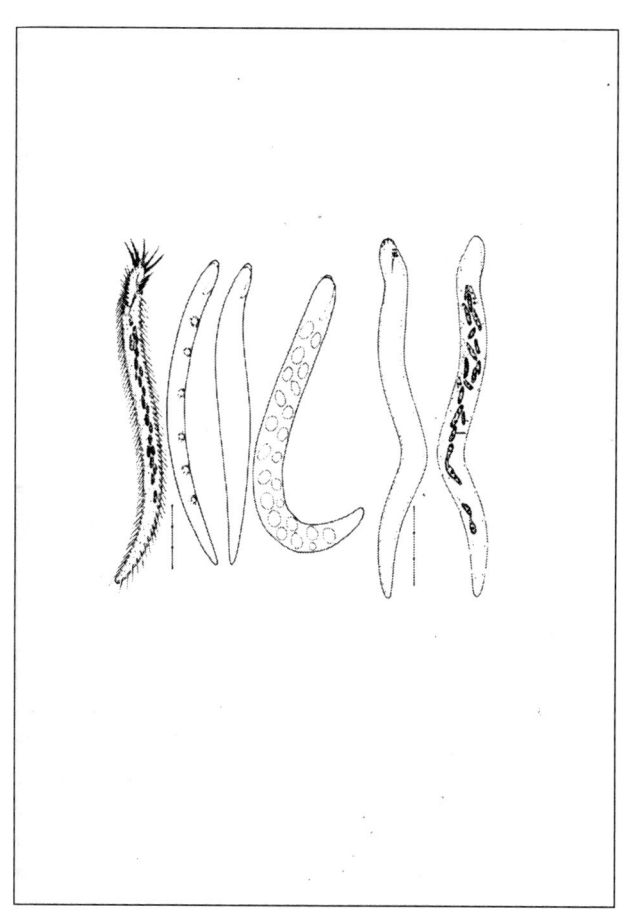

Silent synapse[4]

Ghost owl, death owl, recognizable
by its mask, the silent flight
that is like ours.
Evil omen, devil owl,
spirit with a heart-shaped face,
whose eyes shine blackly
over night fields. Straw owl,
rat owl, whose rasp
doesn't ask a question.
It knows itself and you.
Stone owl, whose stare erases.
It sees you and doesn't care.

---

[4] Aside from the human brain, some of the model systems used for connectomics research are the mouse, the fruit fly, the nematode *C. elegans*, and the barn owl. A silent synapse is one that will not connect in a measurable way.

Infinity[5]

After we exhausted wonder
we shut down the computers, turned off
the lights. Everything
was known. The lab shone
so clean. No dust or grit, no sand
left in the bucket to remind us of the beach.
No wet towels thrown on the floor because we had to
get somewhere right away. The shiny fingerprints
I left on the phone because I couldn't wait
to tell you what would happen next
were gone. We let the air out
of the balloons left over from the surprise party
because there was no more surprise.
We revised the dictionary, took out *curiosity*,
replaced *speculation* with *retrospection*.
We grew our knowledge right up to the end.
When we got to the limit, we stopped.

---

[5] "Someday a fleet of microscopes will capture every neuron and every synapse in a vast database of images, and someday artificially intelligent supercomputers will analyze the images without human assistance, to summarize them in a connectome. I do not know, but I hope that I will live to see that day." – Sebastian Seung, TED Talk *I Am My Connectome*.

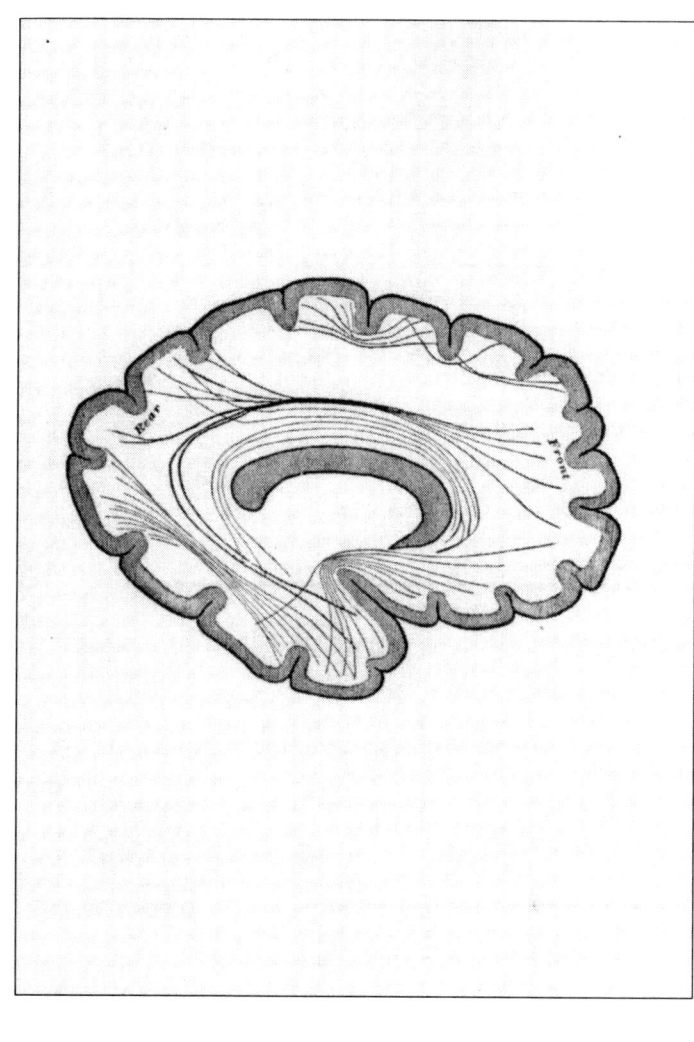

Science[6]

A road, a network, consciousness is
a computer, a map. It's
a vehicle on a road, it's not the road.
It's a stream.
A neuron's like a tree. Consciousness
is a load the vehicle's hauling.
It's water (it's not water). It's a turtle
in a shell, and also it's the shell. It's a
cable, a cord tying things down in a truck box
so they don't fly out.
The brain is like spaghetti, a giant
3D colouring book. You're a kite
and it's the wind. Maybe it's the string.
A synapse is two friends talking on the phone.
The brain's an eavesdropper.
The skull's a box of books you move
from house to house to house.

---

[6] "Let's return from the heights of metaphor, and return to science."
Sebastian Seung, TED Talk *I Am My Connectome*.

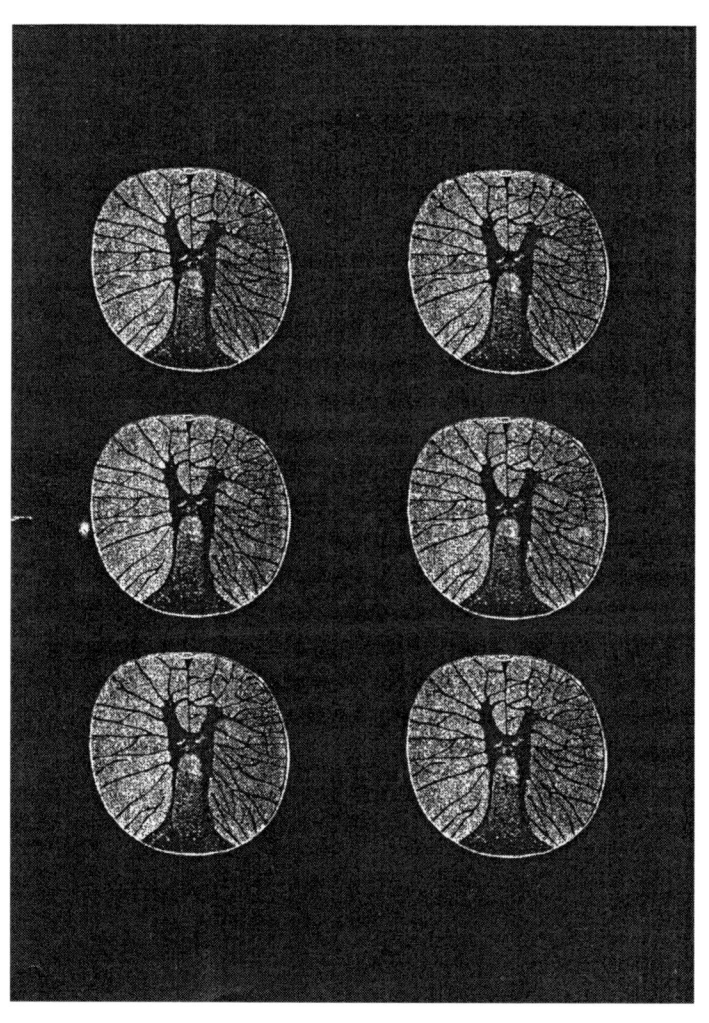

Functional Specialization[7]

The brain is not, as you might think,
a bag of goo.
It is a dense constellation
of carefully mapped drawers.
Here is your speech. Here, your fine motor skills.
Here, the summer you're eleven
and you and your father sit on the dock
watching sheet lightning define the lake's horizon
for what might be hours. It's a hot night;
rough boards scratch your sunburned legs
and catch the seat of your bathing suit.
Later, the storm will turn on you, hailstones
big as eggs breaking the windows
in the back of the cabin, the grass a mess of glass and ice.
But now the storm is far enough away that
there's no thunder, your father's words settling alongside
faint, steady ripples. What he's saying's
not important. The whole sky's a theatre
you watch together.
You've never seen anything like it.

---

[7] Functional specialization suggests that particular areas in the brain control different functions.

A Love Poem: Hebb's Postulate[8]

Cells that fire together,
wire together.

---

[8] Hebb's postulate states that when cells act in concert, the bonds between them are strengthed. Conversely, cells that act at different times show no increased bond strength.

GLIA[9]

After Grandma died, I stripped the sheets from the spare bed
and beneath them found more sheets.
The linen cupboard's layers burst
with threadbare towels, faint traces of old scent.
The sewing room downstairs was packed with scraps,
acrylic yarn left over from the bonnet
in my fat-faced toddler photo, the button jar
an archaeology of fashion.
It was impossible to pack: no suitcase
had a handle or a working latch.
Grandma's thrifty soul exposed, I analyzed,
I diagnosed, drank endless cups of tea
from endless teacups, until
exhausted, heartless, someone called the auctioneer.

Cleaning out her closet, I found a jagged paintline on the wall
where steps used to be. Stairway
to nowhere, plaster and lath below old wallpaper.
My mind tried to rearrange the furniture.
A house could move, not solid but elastic.
The closet was a door, the earth was round,
not flat. As layered as the spare room bed,
the button jar, the other scraps
I'd looked at and discarded.

---

[9] "Glia are the cells that provide support to the neurons. In much the same way that the foundation, framework, walls, and roof of a house provide the structure through which run various electric, cable, and telephone lines,[...] not only do glia provide the structural framework that allows networks of neurons to remain connected, they also attend to the brain's various housekeeping functions (such as removing debris after neuronal death)."
R. Stufflebeam, "Neurons, Synapses, Action Potentials, and Neurotransmission"

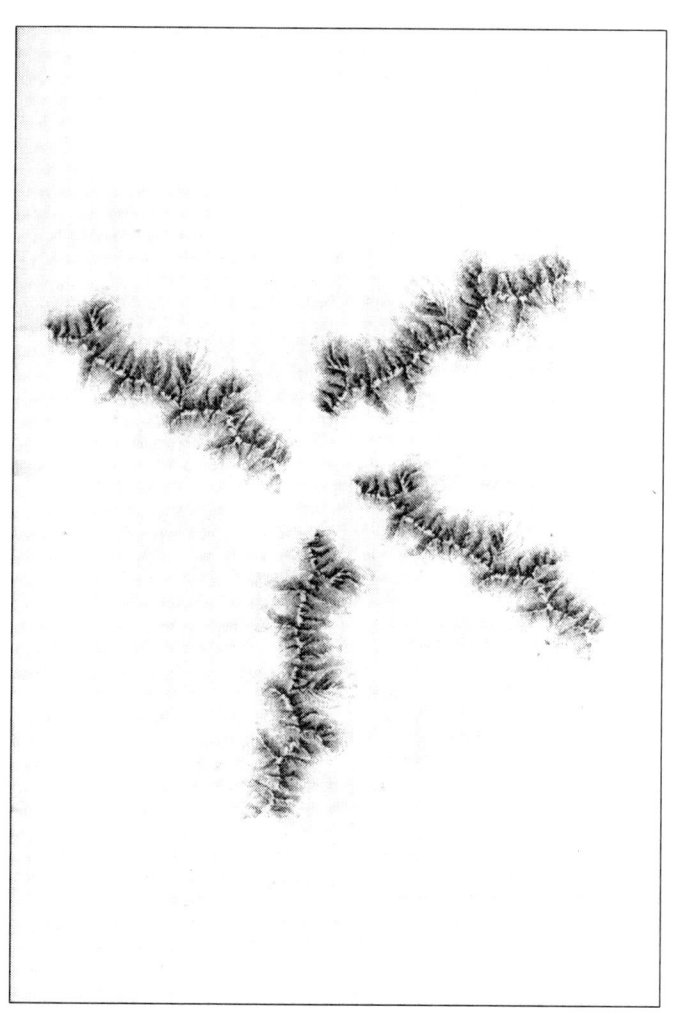

Semantic Selectivity[10]

parents murdered
children convicted

wife killed
husband confessed

children murdered
wife confessed

husband killed
parents convicted

parents killed
children confessed

wife murdered
husband convicted

children killed
husband confessed

husband murdered
parents confessed

---

[10] Brain imaging may allow scientists to chart which parts of the cerebral cortex are active in response to the meaning of particular words. This localized reaction is called semantic selectivity. "For example, on the left-hand side of the brain, above the ear, is one of the tiny regions that represents the word 'victim.' The same region responds to 'killed,' 'convicted,' 'murdered' and 'confessed.' On the brain's right-hand side, near the top of the head, is one of the brain spots activated by family terms: 'wife,' 'husband,' 'children,' 'parents'."

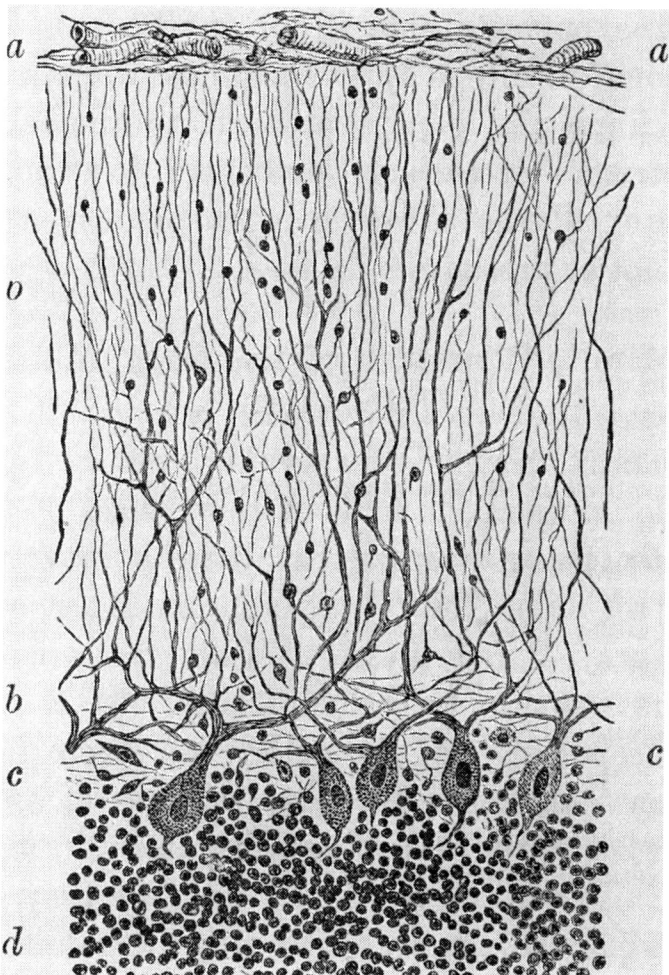

Natural Narrative[11]

Girl in a red hood, with wolf and forest.
Children, orphaned, in the oven.
One beautiful woman trying to kill another.
Truths, they say, the core disguised
as faery. Story growing innocently from itself
like a wick dipped in wax.
Say it again.
The young are cursed by their elders,
animals drive hard bargains.
Story takes on life as flesh fruits around a pit,
tumorous, rotting.
Say how this girl pricks her finger, this one
wants to dance. Her feet cut off.
Strangler story like a vine, glorious,
gangrenous, deliberately unfurling
a glass coffin to show off beauty.
Steal her skin and she'll be yours, say how
when she walks it feels like knives.
Beneath this story is another, and another
under that: nature's ground is shaky,
emperor's clothes threatening to slip.
Say how these truths are like an apple,
with poison at its hollow core.

---

[11] In order to map semantic selectivity, subjects were monitored while they listened to stories described as "natural narratives" for two hours.
A "natural" narrative contains a story's "basic narrative elements such as plot, setting, characterization and speech... [and] has not been manipulated in any premeditated way."

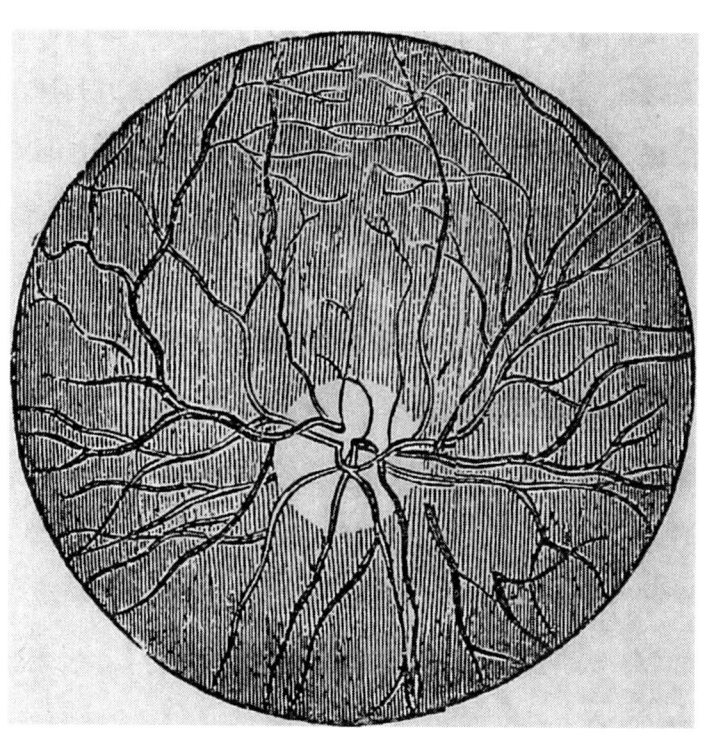

Engram[12]

Memory shimmers, translucent,
just out of reach. The weary traveller,
seeing light in the marsh, yearns for home,
warmth, his mother, bread that steams
when she breaks it, a bowl of milk
waiting beside the white plate, his feet
in their school shoes swinging carefully,
cat purring under his chair, soup heating
on the stove, which is always ready
to dry his mittens, hanging handless
and wet from new snow

even as he thinks that
he's lost, clothes binding, feet sinking,
mud, rocks, reeds reeling him
into breathless embrace.
Will o' the wisp, fool's fire,
you do damage, carrying that torch
to the edge of the precipice,
you kindle the past we think we live in.
Insubstantial, synecdochic,
we're looking for ourselves.
Of course we'll follow you.

---

[12] An engram is the mechanism that stores memory traces as biophysical or biochemical changes in the brain. It is not known exactly where in the brain engrams can be found, and some scientists speculate that the entire brain may be an engram. Engram structure is sometimes explained as being analogous to that of a hologram, in that any part of a hologram contains the whole hologram.

Synaptic Cleft[13]

Awash in neuron surge, chemistry's riptide,
slammed on the sand, yanked back
and thrown, over and over:
it's not easy floating.
Water's a bridge
you can't walk on.
Hung up, flung out: no way
to hurry a slow gate's opening,
hasten the flow. All dams
eventually fail, but an impulse
can't be communicated without resistance.
So dig that hole.
Now: a message in a bottle, and you
without a lifejacket,
current pulling you one way,
down.

---

[13] A synaptic cleft is the small gap between two neurons, across which information passes. Signals from one neuron flow into the gap, and when the gap is flooded, the signal drains into the next neuron. The signal can only flow one direction.

Trials[14]

Fear of home, fear of kitchens,
fear of perfume, fear of spice.
Fear of sun, of light.
Fear of cleaners and soap.
Fear of spring. Fear of green and yellow.
Fear of knives and glasses,
shaving, showers.
Fear of candies, fear of toothpaste,
fear of darkness, fear of dreams.

---

[14] Mapping fear memories can reveal engram location. To create fear memories under controlled conditions, scientists subject patients to electric shocks while introducing unique scents like lemon or mint. Later, scientists monitor the patients' reactions to these scents as the patients sleep.

Wellbutrin™ [15]

Say hello to my little friends,
the blue and white buddies
with whom I take my daily walk.
Pea-sized superheroes, non-caped crusaders,
they save my day, measure my week
in plastic clicks. They put the lid
on the jack-in-the-box, muzzle
the dogs. They keep my umbrella
right side in. Rain or shine,
they've got me.

---

[15] *Wellbutrin* is a brand name for the antidepressant Bupropion.

Flattened Cortex [16]

A grand piano dropped from a window,
the echoing gong of hammers on strings,
all the symphonies all at once:
the ironed brain uncreases.
Thought, released, collides,
the palette of the colour wheel
collapsing into mud.
Metaphors unstack: the poem
is an ocean inside out. How now
describe the nesting doll,
the one inside the one that looks like you?

---

[16] Because the human cortex is so highly folded and layered, it is difficult to read data when it is presented in a 3D model. One way to render this data more readable is to use a computer model to flatten the cortex into two dimensions. Scientific data can then be mapped onto this flat brain.

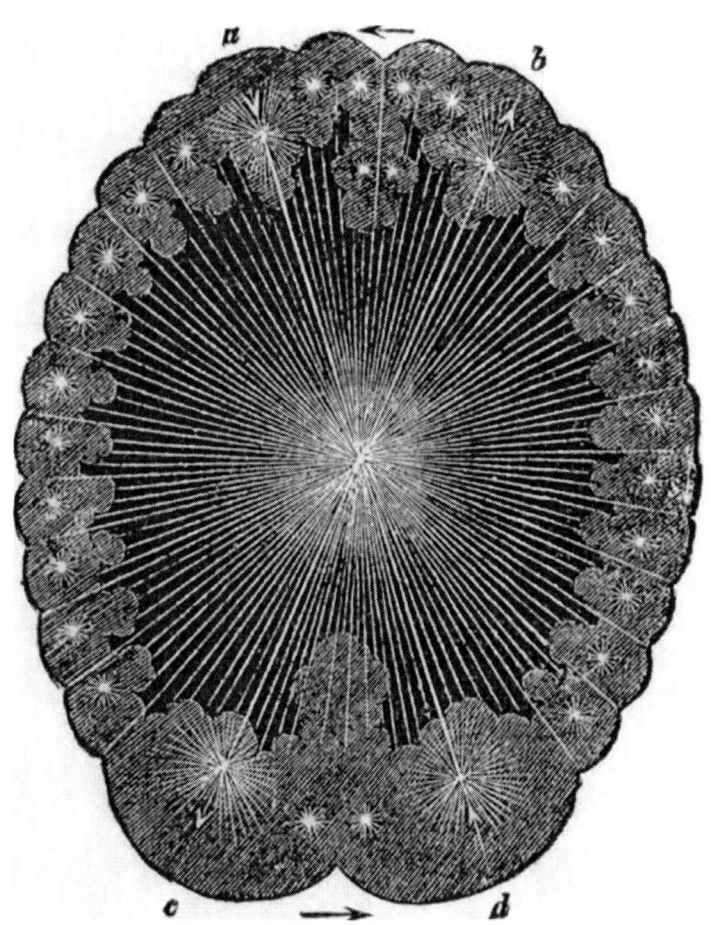

Pycortex [17]

The spare room's quilt is built from scraps,
translucent. Cotton, corduroy, these
are the textures of 1998, when Dad
no longer filled his shirts
and they hung empty in the closet.
Nothing matches. Patches
of stripes, dots, tiny brown triangles
and squares faded to abstraction,
paler versions of themselves
trailing off to nothing.
To make a quilt you layer:
first piece the top, then add the fill and backing.
The quilting is the stitch.
Beneath the squares, the seams are full
of hidden fabric. If you ripped apart
the sutures, laid the fragments side by side,
you could assemble the resemblance
of a blanket, see where it might hold a body.
Pulled back to rags, it won't keep anybody warm.

---

[17] Pycortex is an open source software used to translate information about the brain, specifically that from fMRI and other volumetric data, into a model that is easier to visualize than a traditional 3D map.

NEUROINFORMATICS [18]

The brain's a bin,
a barn, basin
and drain. It's host
and hostage, brim
and lid. Not hammer
nor nail, baby nor pram.
It's net and nib, railing
and stair. Not pail nor rain,
but jailer and jail.

---

[18] Studying the brain generates so much data that regular recording systems can't keep up. Neuroinformatics marries neuroscience and computer science to produce new ways of organizing and understanding the patterns in this dense, quickly moving information.

Optogenetics [19]

Let there be light!
Non-surgical strike, unmanned drone
spiking my skull's desert.
Shot of oil to quiet
the brain's hamster wheel,
settle the pop pop pop
of my bursting thoughts.
Autonomy's not all it's cracked up
to be, surrender now to someone else
flipping the switch, follow
that flashlight's laserbeam.
Tag! I'm it, chasing
the flash, bam!

From beneath, phosphorescent fish
become invisible, their glow melting
into the ocean's plastic underside.
That's what I want, a boneless slide
into camouflage, only reflections
looking in.

---

[19] Optogenetics uses a burst of light to affect genetically sensitized neurons in the brain, so that researchers can manipulate a subject's moods or behaviours.

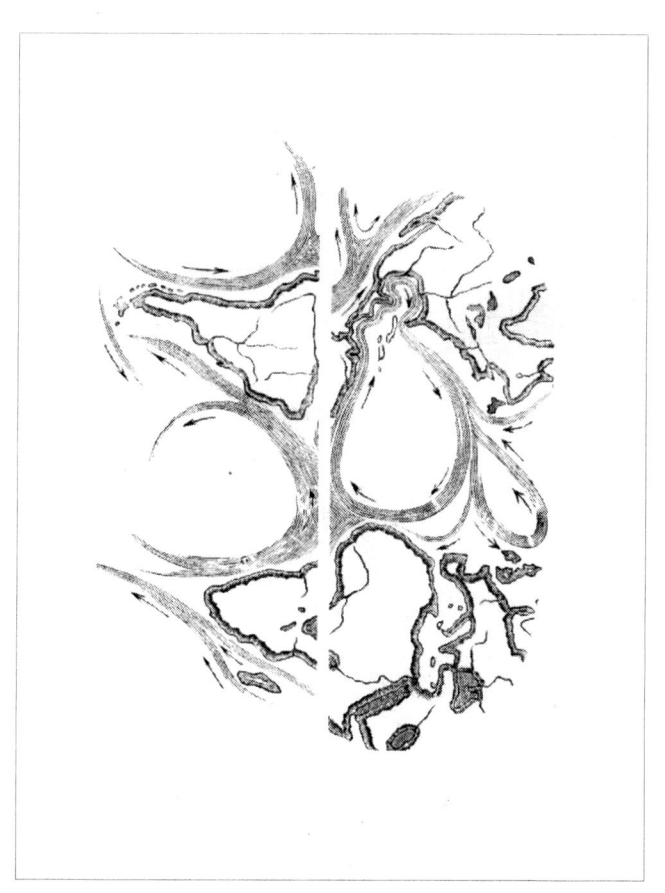

CHIMERA [20]

Autocleave heats,
mousetakes cartograft.
Mark this: in *neuvo*science, it's genedict,
identifraction packed in a spiral suitcase.
Nouveau-logist, embryoidering,
noodling with needles, nuclear
witch graft. New pattern
humonetized:
A N D .

---

[20] A genetic chimera has genetic material that results from combining elements from the DNA from two or more separate fertilized zygotes. A chimera may be produced through genetic manipulation or organ transplantation, among other means. Chimeric mice are an important tool for biological research.

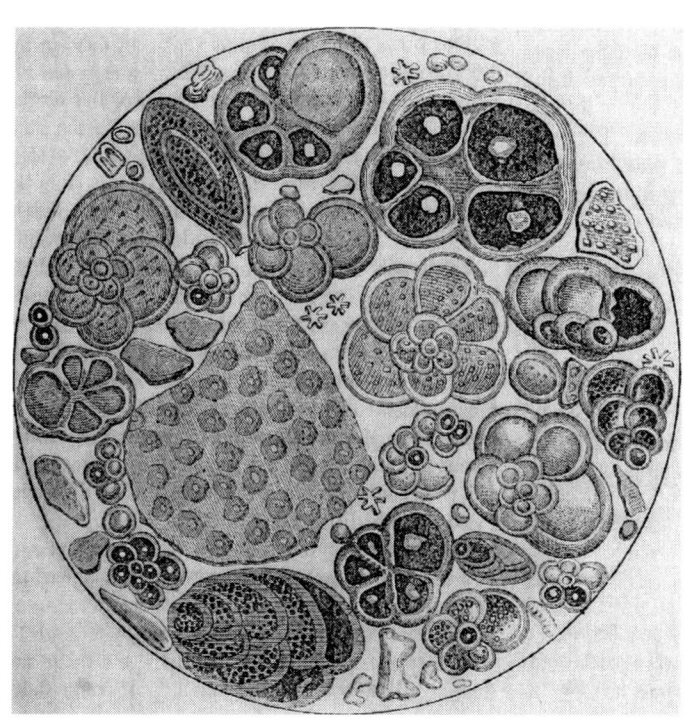

Chimera 2 [21]

When one-eyed Polyphemus asks Odysseus his name,
he answers *no man,*
the original "who's on first?"

Trapped in the cave, Odysseus
speaks monstrously. He is not himself.

To get out of the hole,
he grabs an animal, hangs on.
Polyphemus, groping at the cave's mouth,
feels only beast:
No man has blinded me.

---

[21] In classical Greek mythology, a chimera is a monster made up of a goat, a lion, and a serpent. The word "chimera" also means something that is impossible and cannot exist.

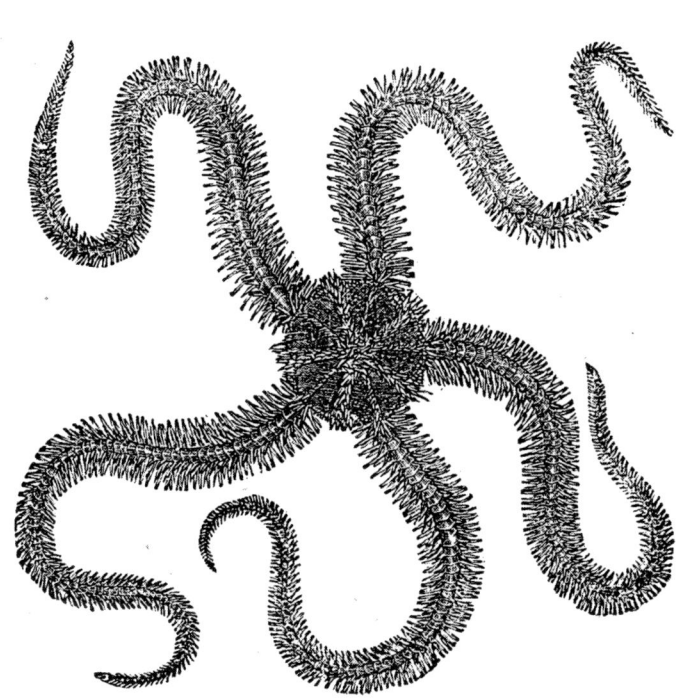

"The Greater Mystery" [22]

Too early to hear pebbles
dropped in the well
or to draw up the sounding line.

Too early to count dogs
barking at 10 pm or lights
coming on over Broadway.

Too early for the chemistry in the cookie,
the hive inside the bees.

Chickens in the eggs, birds
in the hand: not yet. Not time
for haystacks in the needle
and forests in the trees.

Set the alarm and call me when it rings.
I'm going to sleep for a long time.

---

[22] In 2015, John Colapinto interviewed Karl Deisseroth, a leading figure in optogenetics, for *The New Yorker*. "Deisseroth told me that he is no closer to understanding the greater mystery of the mind: how a poem or a piece of music can elicit emotions from a mass of neurons and circuits suspended in fats and water. 'Those are all incredibly important questions,' he said. 'It's just too early to ask them.'"

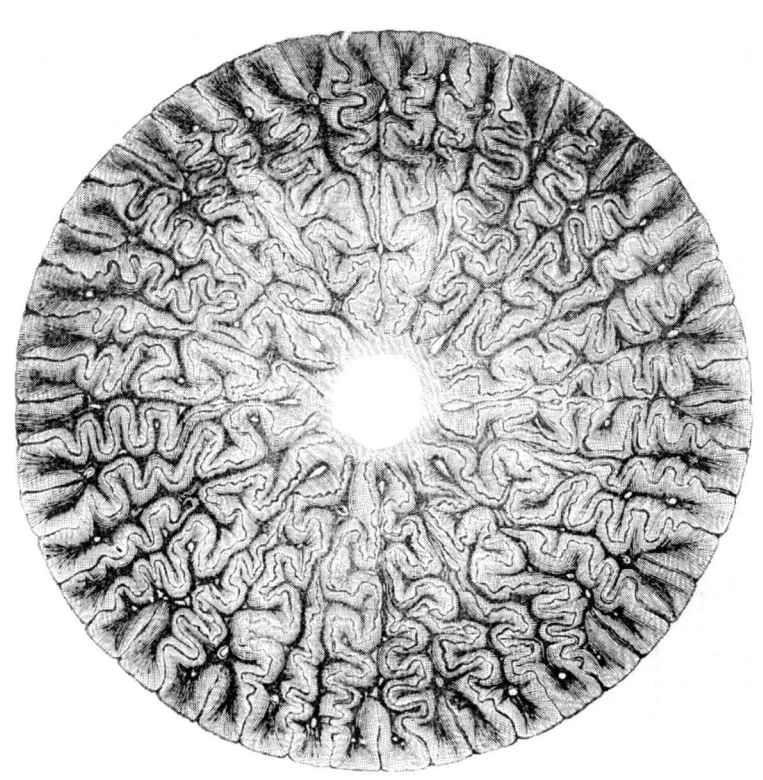

CHLAMYDOMONAS REINHARDTII [23]

Who knew so much of nature
is electric?
Eels, fireflies, the tip
of the iceberg.
Apparently the world is made of light,
that's not a metaphor.
It's a hot mirror getting hotter.
Still, glowing mice don't get too far
outside the lab, spotlit snack
on a midnight flit.
They're not the problem,
the background makes them vulnerable.
We'd never see them
if we flipped a switch, lit up
everything living.

---

[23] *Chlamydomonas reinhardtii*, a single-celled algae, can thrive in total darkness but also has an "eyespot" that senses light. Its entire nuclear genome sequence was published in 2007. It is a model organism for studying how cells respond to light, and was instrumental in the discovery of channelrhodopsin2 (ChR2), which was central to the development of optogenetics.

Lightning Source UK Ltd.
Milton Keynes UK
UKOW03f2358200117
292525UK00002B/77/P